Hands-On Bitcoin Programming with Python

Build powerful online payment centric applications with Python

Harish Kumar Garg

BIRMINGHAM - MUMBAI

Hands-On Bitcoin Programming with Python

Commissioning Editor: Pravin Dhandre
Acquisition Editor: Karan Jain
Content Development Editor: Ronnel Mathew
Technical Editor: Dinesh Pawar
Copy Editor: Safis Editing
Project Coordinator: Nidhi Joshi
Proofreader: Safis Editing
Indexer: Tejal Daruwale Soni
Graphics: Jisha Chirayil
Production Coordinator: Arvindkumar Gupta

First published: August 2018

Production reference: 1280818

Published by Packt Publishing Ltd.
Livery Place
35 Livery Street
Birmingham
B3 2PB, UK.

ISBN 978-1-78953-700-0

www.packtpub.com

mapt.io

Mapt is an online digital library that gives you full access to over 5,000 books and videos, as well as industry leading tools to help you plan your personal development and advance your career. For more information, please visit our website.

Why subscribe?

- Spend less time learning and more time coding with practical eBooks and Videos from over 4,000 industry professionals

- Improve your learning with Skill Plans built especially for you

- Get a free eBook or video every month

- Mapt is fully searchable

- Copy and paste, print, and bookmark content

PacktPub.com

Did you know that Packt offers eBook versions of every book published, with PDF and ePub files available? You can upgrade to the eBook version at www.PacktPub.com and as a print book customer, you are entitled to a discount on the eBook copy. Get in touch with us at service@packtpub.com for more details.

At www.PacktPub.com, you can also read a collection of free technical articles, sign up for a range of free newsletters, and receive exclusive discounts and offers on Packt books and eBooks.

Contributors

About the author

Harish Kumar Garg founder of BignumWorks Software LLP, is a data scientist and a lead software developer with 17 years' experience in the software industry. BignumWorks Software LLP is an India-based software consultancy that provides consultancy services in the area of software development and technical training. Harish has worked for McAfee and Intel for over 11 years. He is an expert in creating data visualizations using R, Python, and web-based visualization libraries.

Packt is searching for authors like you

If you're interested in becoming an author for Packt, please visit `authors.packtpub.com` and apply today. We have worked with thousands of developers and tech professionals, just like you, to help them share their insight with the global tech community. You can make a general application, apply for a specific hot topic that we are recruiting an author for, or submit your own idea.

Table of Contents

Preface

In this book, you will be introduced to Bitcoin and Blockchain, and how to take part in the Bitcoin ecosystem. You will learn about Bitcoin and its features, Blockchain, and how both can work together. You'll also learn how to use Pi Bitcoin tools to program Bitcoin with Python. You will learn about interacting with Blockchain APIs programmatically with Python, and about Bitcoin mining and how to get started with it. We will also explore Bitcoin trading bots. This book also deals with exploring and analyzing the tremendous amount of data being generated in the Bitcoin ecosystem; how to get, clean, manipulate, and visualize Bitcoin price data; and how to analyze a Bitcoin dice game's data using Python's data analysis tools.

What this book covers

Chapter 1, *Getting Started with Bitcoin*, introduces Bitcoin and Blockchain, and how to take part in the Bitcoin ecosystem. We will learn about Bitcoin and its features, Blockchain, how both work together, and what the differences between them are. Also, we will explore how to get a Bitcoin wallet and how to start using it, along with how to send and spend Bitcoin.

Chapter 2, *Programming Bitcoin and Blockchain with Python*, explores Bitcoin and Blockchain API's programmatically. Also, we will learn how to get started with mining Bitcoin.

Chapter 3, *Earning Bitcoin Programmatically*, demonstrates how to start accepting Bitcoin as a payment method. We will also learn how to build and sell API-based microservices to earn Bitcoin and explore Bitcoin trading bots.

Chapter 4, *Bitcoin Data Analysis*, explores and analyzes the tremendous amount of data being generated in the Bitcoin ecosystem.

To get the most out of this book

Anyone with some Python experience who wants to explore Python Bitcoin programming and start building Bitcoin-driven Python apps will benefit from this book.

Download the example code files

You can download the example code files for this book from your account at `www.packtpub.com`. If you purchased this book elsewhere, you can visit `www.packtpub.com/support` and register to have the files emailed directly to you.

You can download the code files by following these steps:

1. Log in or register at `www.packtpub.com`.
2. Select the **SUPPORT** tab.
3. Click on **Code Downloads & Errata**.
4. Enter the name of the book in the **Search** box and follow the onscreen instructions.

Once the file is downloaded, please make sure that you unzip or extract the folder using the latest version of:

- WinRAR/7-Zip for Windows
- Zipeg/iZip/UnRarX for Mac
- 7-Zip/PeaZip for Linux

The code bundle for the book is also hosted on GitHub at `https://github.com/PacktPublishing/Hands-On-Bitcoin-Programming-with-Python`. In case there's an update to the code, it will be updated on the existing GitHub repository.

We also have other code bundles from our rich catalog of books and videos available at `https://github.com/PacktPublishing/`. Check them out!

Download the color images

We also provide a PDF file that has color images of the screenshots/diagrams used in this book. You can download it here: `https://www.packtpub.com/sites/default/files/downloads/HandsOnBitcoinProgrammingwithPython_ColorImages.pdf`.

Conventions used

There are a number of text conventions used throughout this book.

`CodeInText`: Indicates code words in text, database table names, folder names, filenames, file extensions, pathnames, dummy URLs, user input, and Twitter handles. Here is an example: "Create three public keys from those private keys using the `privtopub` function."

A block of code is set as follows:

```
# Generate Public Key
my_public_key = privtopub(my_private_key)
print("Public Key: %s\n" % my_public_key)
```

Any command-line input or output is written as follows:

```
pip install bitcoin
```

Bold: Indicates a new term, an important word, or words that you see onscreen. For example, words in menus or dialog boxes appear in the text like this. Here is an example: "The screenshot shows the statistical data (**DATA | Stats**)"

Warnings or important notes appear like this.

Tips and tricks appear like this.

Get in touch

Feedback from our readers is always welcome.

General feedback: Email `feedback@packtpub.com` and mention the book title in the subject of your message. If you have questions about any aspect of this book, please email us at `questions@packtpub.com`.

Errata: Although we have taken every care to ensure the accuracy of our content, mistakes do happen. If you have found a mistake in this book, we would be grateful if you would report this to us. Please visit `www.packtpub.com/submit-errata`, selecting your book, clicking on the Errata Submission Form link, and entering the details.

Piracy: If you come across any illegal copies of our works in any form on the Internet, we would be grateful if you would provide us with the location address or website name. Please contact us at copyright@packtpub.com with a link to the material.

If you are interested in becoming an author: If there is a topic that you have expertise in and you are interested in either writing or contributing to a book, please visit authors.packtpub.com.

Reviews

Please leave a review. Once you have read and used this book, why not leave a review on the site that you purchased it from? Potential readers can then see and use your unbiased opinion to make purchase decisions, we at Packt can understand what you think about our products, and our authors can see your feedback on their book. Thank you!

For more information about Packt, please visit packtpub.com.

1
Getting Started with Bitcoin

This chapter focuses on bitcoin, its features, and how can we take part in the bitcoin ecosystem. The bitcoin ecosystem runs by its users getting, spending, and sending bitcoin wallets. In order to understand the concepts of this chapter, you should have at least a basic understanding of the command line on the computer you're using, and you should have Python 3.x installed on your computer.

In this chapter, we will look at the following topics:

- Introducing bitcoin and its features
- Introducing blockchain
- Attributes of bitcoin and blockchain
- How to get a bitcoin wallet
- The different forms of bitcoin wallet including getting, sending, and spending

Introduction to bitcoin and blockchains

In this section, we will explore the following topics:

- Bitcoin
- The uses of bitcoin
- Blockchains
- Attributes of bitcoin and blockchain

What is bitcoin?

Bitcoin is a digital currency. This means that it exists only as an electronic record, and, unlike physical currency, you cannot hold it in your hand. You can send and receive money using bitcoin (just as you can with other methods), as well as pay for things and services with bitcoin. Bitcoin is interchangeable with traditional money.

There are exchanges where you can buy and sell bitcoin. There are many other digital currencies, but bitcoin is the first and the most popular. Bitcoin uses peer-to-peer technology to operate, with no central authority or banks managing transactions, and the issuing of bitcoin is carried out collectively by the network.

Bitcoin is open source—its design is public; nobody owns or controls bitcoin, and everybody can use it. Bitcoin is digital and decentralized. For the first time in history, people can exchange value without intermediaries, which translates to greater control of funds and lower fees.

It's a cryptocurrency, which means it's secured by design.

Uses of bitcoin

There are a lot of advantages to using bitcoin. Some of them are as follows:

- **Fast and easy payments**: It's extremely easy and fast to make payments with bitcoin. You do not have to worry about which software to use. The bitcoin network never sleeps, even on holidays. Sending payments internationally is also very easy; there are no banks to make anyone wait three business days, no extra fees for making an international transfer, and no special limitations on the minimum or maximum amount one can send.
- **Privacy**: Payment can be made using bitcoin without sharing any personal info; one does not need to sign up or share any card information. In fact, it is even possible to send a payment without revealing one's identity, almost like you can with physical money. However, take note that some effort may be required to protect privacy.
- **Negligible transaction fees**: There are very little or minimal transaction fees while making payments with bitcoin. There are no fees to receive bitcoins, and having many wallets allows you to control how large a fee to pay when spending. Most wallets have reasonable default fees, and higher fees can encourage faster confirmation of your transactions. Fees are unrelated to the amount transferred, so it's possible to send 100,000 bitcoins for the same fee it costs to send one bitcoin.
- **Secure**: Bitcoins are created and held electronically, but there is no credit card number involved that someone can steal as nobody can charge you money on your behalf. The transactions are made using military-grade cryptography and are highly confidential. Bitcoin will provide full access over your money and a high level of protection against almost all types of fraudulent works which involves certain steps.

- **Multisignature**: Bitcoin's multisignature feature allows businesses full control over their spending by allowing bitcoins to be spent only if a subset of a group of people authorize the transaction.
- **Great for developers**: For developers, bitcoin is the simplest of all payment systems. There are many third-party payment processing services that provide APIs. We don't need to store bitcoins on our server. If you don't use any third-party APIs, you can integrate a bitcoin node directly into your applications, allowing it to become your own bank and payment processor.

What is a blockchain?

In simple terms, a blockchain is a digital ledger. It's a public record of bitcoin transactions arranged in chronological order. It is a permissionless, distributed database based on the bitcoin protocol that maintains a continuously growing list of transactional data records. It is distributed so that each participant has the copy of the whole blockchain. The blockchain is shared between all bitcoin users.

It is used to verify the permanence of bitcoin transactions and to prevent double spending. It is secure and immutable, and it's also hardened against tampering and revision, even by operators of the data store's nodes.

Each blockchain record is enforced cryptographically, and hosts run machines working as data store nodes. A blockchain is made up of blocks. A block is a record in the blockchain that contains and confirms many waiting transactions, as shown at `https://www.blockchain.com/explorer`:

Roughly every ten minutes, a new block containing transactions is appended to the blockchain through mining. It is a file called the bitcoin blockchain sitting on thousands of computers across the world, perhaps even on your own PC at home. The file contains data about all bitcoin transactions—that is, the payment of bitcoins from one account to another—that have ever happened.

This is often called a **ledger**, and is similar to a bank ledger, which keeps a record of payments.

Attributes of bitcoin and blockchain

Both bitcoin and blockchains have the following similar attributes:

- Blockchain is the technology behind bitcoin. It works like a database for all bitcoin transactions, and it keeps all records of bitcoin transactions since the very first transaction. The initial and most widely known application of blockchain technology was the public ledger of transactions for bitcoin. However, digital currencies are not the only use for blockchain technology.
- Blockchain is a no-trust-based system, which can be used to conduct all kinds of transactions, such as digital contract signing. blockchain technology can be used to create a permanent public transparent ledger system for compiling data on sales, storing rights data by authenticating copyright registration, and so on.

 There is even a digital nation founded on blockchain technology, called **Bitnation**.

Getting a bitcoin wallet

To start making payments with bitcoin, we need a bitcoin wallet. However, before we create a wallet, we should be aware of the following things:

- **Security**: We should take steps to secure our wallet. There are a lot of different features that come with different wallets. You should evaluate all of them and choose whichever is best for you.
- **Volatility**: The bitcoin price is volatile and goes up and down, depending on market conditions.

There are a few more things that you need to be aware of. For more information, refer to `https://bitcoin.org/en/you-need-to-know`.

The different forms of bitcoin wallet

Bitcoin wallets come in a lot of different forms. Some of them are listed here:

- There are smartphone app wallets, there are online web wallets—for example, blockchain.info and coinbase.info—there are desktop-based wallets for macOS, Linux, and Windows operating systems, and there are also dedicated hardware-based wallets.
- Online web wallets can be accessed from any web browser and from any operating system, so that makes it quite platform-independent:
    - One of the most popular ones is coinbase.info, where you can purchase and send bitcoins.
    - There are a few others as well, such as BitGo, BTC.com, Coin.Space, GreenAddress, and so on. There are also mobile wallets that you can use from your smartphone. They are available for Android phones, Windows phones, Blackberries, and iOS phones. Some of the most popular ones are breadwallet, Coin.Space, Mycelium, and so on.
- There are also wallets that are available for desktop computers running on all operating systems. Some of the popular ones are bitcoin Core, GreenAddress, and BitGo, among others.
- Bitcoin wallets may require specific hardware solutions, for example, Trezor. Trezor is a hardware wallet that has a lot more security, and we can even sign transactions, connect to an online device, and spend bitcoins from this wallet. It is a separate device, so it's much more secure and less prone to hacking. It is also recommended that you use bitcoin cold storage for a large number of bitcoins. Bitcoin cold storage can be held offline, like in a paper-money wallet. For this purpose, you can get a bitcoin address from `bitaddress.org`, which can be used to send bitcoins and then store the details offline.

Getting and sending bitcoins

Bitcoins can be bought from an exchange website. One example of an exchange website is Coinbase.info, and bitcoin.org lists a lot of these exchange websites. Some operate globally and some are specific to a particular country or a region, depending on the laws of that country. There are exchanges available for all regions and countries of the world. For example, one of the most popular ones is Coinbase.com. Here, bitcoins can be sent and sold, and you can see your account details, containing information on what bitcoins you hold with them.

You can also buy bitcoins from bitcoin ATMs. One of the best websites to use to find your local bitcoin ATM is `https://coinatmradar.com/`. For example, the following screenshot shows a map of the United States, where you can see all the available bitcoin ATMs where you can buy bitcoin:

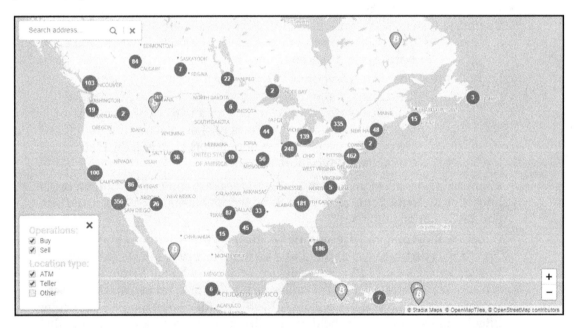

You can also buy bitcoins in person from other users. The locations of people who are interested in selling bitcoins can be found at `https://localbitcoins.com/`. In the following screenshot, we can see all the people in the United States who are interested in selling bitcoins. Bitcoins can be bought from this site by other users. You can also sell bitcoins to other users who are interested in buying them:

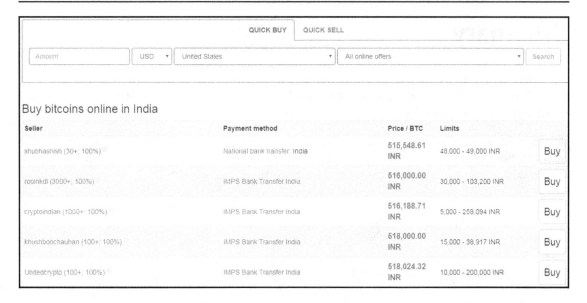

Buy bitcoins online in India

Seller	Payment method	Price / BTC	Limits	
shubhashish (30+; 100%)	National bank transfer. India	515,548.61 INR	48,000 - 49,000 INR	Buy
robinkdl (3000+; 100%)	IMPS Bank Transfer India	516,000.00 INR	30,000 - 103,200 INR	Buy
cryptoindian (1000+; 100%)	IMPS Bank Transfer India	516,188.71 INR	5,000 - 258,094 INR	Buy
khushboochauhan (100+; 100%)	IMPS Bank Transfer India	518,000.00 INR	15,000 - 38,917 INR	Buy
Unitedcrypto (100+; 100%)	IMPS Bank Transfer India	518,024.32 INR	10,000 - 200,000 INR	Buy

There are also a lot of places where we can spend bitcoins online on products and services. One of the sites to find these places is `https://spendabit.co/`. From this site, we can search for the products from sellers who accept bitcoins as payment.

For example, when we perform a sample search of toaster in the search bar, it will show all the listings from the sellers who are selling this product and are ready to accept bitcoins as payment.

Another place to find businesses that accept bitcoins is `http://99bitcoins.com`. This website contains a list of companies that accept bitcoins as payment. There are a lot of well-known names that are listed, as shown in the following list:

- **WordPress**: Allows people to create blogs
- **Overstock**: The online retailer
- **Subway**: Accepts bitcoins
- **Microsoft**: Users can buy content with bitcoin on Windows store
- **Reddit**: Buy premium features with bitcoins

If you are interested in searching for local businesses that accept bitcoins, you can search for them at coinmap.org.

Summary

In this chapter, we were introduced to bitcoin and blockchain technology, and how we can start playing a part in the bitcoin ecosystem. We learned about bitcoin and its features, blockchains, how bitcoin and blockchains work together, and what the difference between them is. We also explored getting a bitcoin wallet and how to start using it.

We learned how to get and send bitcoins, and we learned about the various places to get bitcoins, both online and offline. We looked at how to send bitcoins, and we looked at some places where you can spend bitcoins and buy products and services.

In the next chapter, we will explore the bitcoin and blockchain APIs programmatically, and look at how to get started with mining bitcoins.

2
Programming Bitcoin and Blockchain with Python

This chapter focuses on using Raspberry Pi Bitcoin tools to program bitcoin with Python and interacting with Blockchain APIs programmatically. The reader will also get a general idea of the process of mining bitcoin and its initial stages.

In this chapter, we will learn about the following topics:

- Programming bitcoin using Python
- Creating a multisignature bitcoin address
- Blockchain API programming with Python
- Installing the Blockchain.info
- Python library
- Learning to mine bitcoin
- How to mine bitcoin
- Increasing difficulties in mining bitcoins

Programming bitcoin with Python

In this section, we are going to introduce the following topics:

- The Raspberry Pi Bitcoin tools library and how to start using it
- How to generate private keys and public keys
- How to create a simple bitcoin address from the private keys and public keys you generated

To get started with bitcoin using Python, you must install Python 3.x and the bitcoin Python library called Pi Bitcoin tools in the system.

Pi Bitcoin tools library

To install the Pi Bitcoin tools library, open the command-line program and execute the following command:

```
pip install bitcoin
```

The best thing about this library is that it does not need to have a bitcoin node on your computer in order for you to start using it.

This library connects to the bitcoin network and pulls data from places such as Blockchain.info.

We shall start by writing the equivalent of a `Hello World` program for bitcoin in Python. In the `hello_bitcoin.py` script, the demonstration of a new bitcoin address is created using Python.

Go through the following steps to run the program:

1. Import the bitcoin library:

    ```
    #!/usr/bin/env python
    '''
    Title - Hello Bitcoin
    This program demonstrates the creation of
    - private key,
    - public key
    - and a bitcoin address.
    '''

    # import bitcoin
    from bitcoin import *
    ```

2. Generate a private key using the random key function:

    ```
    my_private_key = random_key()
    ```

3. Display the private key on the screen:

```
print("Private Key: %s\n" % my_private_key)
```

How to generate private keys and public keys

With the private key, a public key is generated. Perform this step by passing the private key that was generated to the `privtopub` function, as shown here:

```
# Generate Public Key
my_public_key = privtopub(my_private_key)
print("Public Key: %s\n" % my_public_key)
```

Now, with the public key, generate a bitcoin address. Do this by passing the public key that is generated to the `pubtoaddr` function:

```
# Create a bitcoin address
my_bitcoin_address = pubtoaddr(my_public_key)
print("Bitcoin Address: %s\n" % my_bitcoin_address)
```

The following screenshot shows the private key, public key and bitcoin address that is generated:

Bitcoin address

A bitcoin address is a single-use token. Just as people use email addresses to send and receive emails, you can use this bitcoin address to send and receive bitcoins. Unlike email addresses, however, people have many different bitcoin addresses, and a unique address should be used for each transaction.

Creating a multisignature bitcoin address

A multisignature address is an address that is associated with more than one private key; therefore, we need to create three private keys.

Go through the following steps to create a multisignature bitcoin address:

1. Create three private keys:

```
#!/usr/bin/env python
'''
Title - Create multi-signature address

This program demonstrates the creation of
Multi-signature bitcoin address.
'''
# import bitcoin
from bitcoin import *

# Create Private Keys
my_private_key1 = random_key()
my_private_key2 = random_key()
my_private_key3 = random_key()

print("Private Key1: %s" % my_private_key1)
print("Private Key2: %s" % my_private_key2)
print("Private Key3: %s" % my_private_key3)
print('\n')
```

2. Create three public keys from those private keys using the `privtopub` function:

```
# Create Public keys
my_public_key1 = privtopub(my_private_key1)
my_public_key2 = privtopub(my_private_key2)
my_public_key3 = privtopub(my_private_key3)

print("Public Key1: %s" % my_public_key1)
print("Public Key2: %s" % my_public_key2)
print("Public Key3: %s" % my_public_key3)
print('\n')
```

3. After generating the public keys, create the `multisig` by passing the three public keys to the `mk_ multi-sig_script` function. The resulting `multisig` is passed to the `addr` script function to create the multisignature bitcoin address.

```
# Create Multi-signature address
my_multi_sig = mk_multisig_script(my_private_key1, my_private_key2,
my_private_key3, 2,3)
my_multi_address = scriptaddr(my_multi_sig)
print("Multi signature address: %s" % my_multi_address)
```

4. Print the multisignature address and execute the script.

The following screenshot shows the output for the `multisig` bitcoin address:

Multisignature addresses are useful in organizations where no single individual is trusted with authorising the spending of bitcoins.

You can also look at the preexisting bitcoin addresses' transactional history. We will first get a valid address from Blockchain.info.

The following screenshot shows the copied address of a bitcoin block:

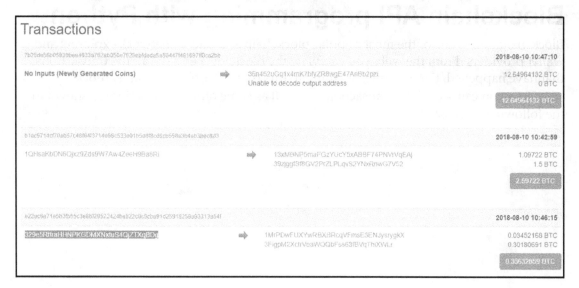

Pass the copied address to the `history` function, as shown in the following code, along with the output to get the history of the bitcoin address, including the transactional information:

```
!/usr/bin/env python
'''
Title - Bitcoin Transaction History

This program demonstrates listing history of a bitcoin address.
'''
# import bitcoin
from bitcoin import *

#View address transaction history
a_valid_bitcoin_address = '329e5RtfraHHNPKGDMXNxtuS4QjZTXqBDg'
print(history(a_valid_bitcoin_address))
```

```
C:\WINDOWS\system32\cmd.exe                                    —  □  ×

C:\Users\test\Desktop\11520>python history.py
[{'address': '329e5RtfraHHNPKGDMXNxtuS4QjZTXqBDg', 'value': 33769275, 'output': 'a09bc970853bd3acc1e3d6ca53edcaa4ecb0c48
aa8df6f49a7a9b50e09cd8a1b:1', 'block_height': 536072, 'spend': 'e22ac6a71e5b3fb55c3e8bf29522424ba822c0c5cba91d25918259a9
3313a54f:0'}]
```

Blockchain API programming with Python

Blockchain.info is one of the most popular blockchain and bitcoin network explorers and wallet providers. From the web, you can view the block level and see all the transactions that have happened. For example, by going to this particular block—that is, **Block #536081**—you can see all the transactions, as well as some other information, as shown in the following screenshot:

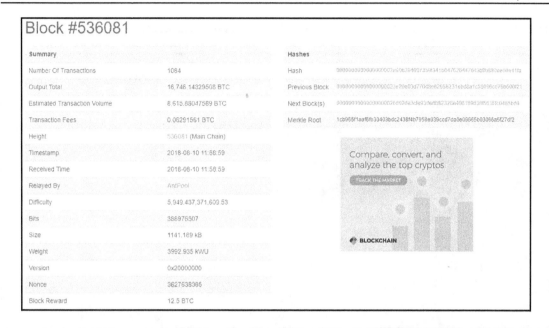

Block #536081

Summary		Hashes	
Number Of Transactions	1084	Hash	00000000000000000007a90b28460735983415647626447643b0b8802ee04e1fa
Output Total	16,746.14329508 BTC	Previous Block	0000000089600000023e20e03d770dbe82658231ebd8a1c68096cd75b600f21
Estimated Transaction Volume	8,615.88047589 BTC	Next Block(s)	0000000090000000026d92da3de950e6bbf2328a408189838f56351c0485bd0
Transaction Fees	0.06291561 BTC	Merkle Root	1cb965f1aaf6fb30403bdc2438f4b7958e039ccd7da0e09665b03066a5f27df2
Height	536081 (Main Chain)		
Timestamp	2018-08-10 11:58:59		
Received Time	2018-08-10 11:58:59		
Relayed By	AntPool		
Difficulty	5,949,437,371,609.53		
Bits	388976507		
Size	1141.189 kB		
Weight	3992.935 kWU		
Version	0x20000000		
Nonce	3627638085		
Block Reward	12.5 BTC		

Compare, convert, and analyze the top cryptos

TRACK THE MARKET

BLOCKCHAIN

The following screenshot shows the statistical data (**DATA | Stats**). This is great, and useful as well; however, for a developer building applications or performing analysis based on this data, it is important to get this data programmatically:

Bitcoin Stats

Summary of bitcoin statistics for the previous 24 hour period.

BLOCK SUMMARY

Blocks Mined	149
Time Between Blocks	9.21 minutes
Bitcoins Mined	1,862.50000000 BTC

MARKET SUMMARY

Market Price	$6,396.51	View Chart
Trade Volume	$482,316,162.23	
Trade Volume	75,891.60000000 BTC	

TRANSACTION SUMMARY

Total Transaction Fees (BTC)	21.77783945 BTC	View Chart
Number of Transactions	221,755	View Chart
Total Output Volume (BTC)	1,080,665.47279284 BTC	View Chart
Estimated Transaction Volume (BTC)	147,471.53013832 BTC	View Chart

The following screenshot shows the market data (**DATA | Markets**):

Installing the Blockchain.info Python library

The following are the steps to install the `blockchain` Python library:

1. Open the command-line program on your computer.
2. Run the `pip install blockchain` command to install the `blockchain` library.

   The following screenshot shows the installation of bitcoin:

Getting bitcoin exchange rates from Blockchain.info

The following steps shows the method for bitcoin exchange rates:

1. First, import the `exchangerates` classes from the `blockchain` library:

```
#!/usr/bin/env python

# import blockchain library
from blockchain import exchangerates
```

2. Exchange rates define a `get_ticker` method, which returns the exchange rates data in a dictionary object. Call this method and save the resulting object. The `ticker` dictionary object that we have has currency symbols as keys:

```
# get the Bitcoin rates in various currencies
ticker = exchangerates.get_ticker()
```

3. By running over these keys, data about the various rates can be pulled. For example, the latest bitcoin rates can be obtained in each currency by getting the `p15min` minimum value:

```
# print the Bitcoin price for every currency
print("Bitcoin Prices in various currencies:")
for k in ticker:
 print(k, ticker[k].p15min)
```

The following screenshot shows the list of currencies and the equivalent bitcoin rate for those currencies at that moment or from the last 15 minutes:

```
Select C:\WINDOWS\system32\cmd.exe

C:\Users\test\Desktop\11520>python get_exchange_rates.py
Bitcoin Prices in various currencies:
USD 6473.09
AUD 8854.02
BRL 24606.34
CAD 8478.07
CHF 6436.94
CLP 4188478.45
CNY 44362.38
DKK 42119.5
EUR 5654.4
GBP 5069.95
HKD 50814.09
INR 445576.75
ISK 703900.92
JPY 717353.48
KRW 7300999.67
NZD 9809.48
PLN 24232.78
RUB 433159.85
SEK 58869.77
SGD 8872.73
THB 215320.91
TWD 198775.11
```

A particular currency can also be converted to bitcoin. For example, you can pass the `to_btc` method and pass in the currency and the amount that we want to convert to `btc`, and get the result as bitcoin. The following code shows how to do this for a value of 100 euros:

```
# Getting Bitcoin value for a particular amount and currency
btc = exchangerates.to_btc('EUR', 100)
print("\n100 euros in Bitcoin: %s " % btc)
```

The following screenshot shows the output for 100 euros in bitcoin:

```
100 euros in Bitcoin: 0.01769439
```

Statistics

The next class from the bitcoin blockchain library is called `statistics`.

There are a number of methods that can be called to get a wide variety of blockchain stats data, for example, as shown in the following screenshot:

```
Stats

    trade_volume_btc : float
    miners_revenue_usd : float
    btc_mined : long
    trade_volume_usd : float
    difficulty : float
    minutes_between_blocks : float
    number_of_transactions : int
    hash_rate : float
    timestamp : long
    mined_blocks : int
    blocks_size : int
    total_fees_btc : int
    total_btc_sent : long
    estimated_btc_sent : long
    total_btc : long
    total_blocks :int
    next_retarget : int
    estimated_transaction_volume_usd : float
    miners_revenue_btc : int
    market_price_usd : float
```

You can call the different methods as follows:

- Import the relevant class, call the `get` method on `statistics`, and save that object. For example, to get the bitcoin trade volume, we should get the `trade_volume_btc` property from the `stats` object that was created, as shown in the following code:

```
#!/usr/bin/env python

# import blockchain library
from blockchain import statistics

# get the stats object
stats = statistics.get()

# get and print Bitcoin trade volume
print("Bitcoin Trade Volume: %s\n" % stats.trade_volume_btc)
```

The following screenshot shows the bitcoin trade volume:

```
Select C:\WINDOWS\system32\cmd.exe

C:\Users\test\Desktop\11520>python get_stats.py
Bitcoin Trade Volume: 75891.6
```

- To get the total bitcoins mined, call the `btc_mined` property on `stats` object, as shown here:

```
# get and print Bitcoin mined
print("Bitcoin mined: %s\n" % stats.btc_mined)
```

The following screenshot shows the output of the number of bitcoins mined:

```
Bitcoin mined: 191250000000
```

- To get the bitcoin market price, use the `stats` class, call the market price and append that with the particular currency:

```
# get and print Bitcoin market price in usd
print("Bitcoin market price: %s\n" % stats.market_price_usd)
```

- The current bitcoin price is shown in US dollars as follows:

```
Bitcoin market price: 6355.33
```

Block explorer methods

For block explorer methods, start by importing the relevant classes from the `blockchain` library. To get a particular block, call the `get_block` method as shown in the following code. It expects a block to be passed in as the parameter.

```
# import blockchain library
from blockchain import blockexplorer

# get a particular block
block = blockexplorer.get_block('')
```

By taking an example block from the web, from Blockchain.info, copy the hash for this block (**Block #536081**) and pass it to the `get_block` method, as shown in the following screenshot:

Block #536081

Summary		Hashes	
Number Of Transactions	1084	Hash	0000000000000000002e90b284607359f3415647626447643b9b880ee00e41fa
Output Total	16,746.14329508 BTC	Previous Block	0000000000000000023e20e03d770d8a82656231ebd8a1c85096cd79b680f21
Estimated Transaction Volume	8,615.88047589 BTC	Next Block(s)	0000000000000000026d92de3cfe93dedb82328a48318903815635fc0465bd0
Transaction Fees	0.06291561 BTC	Merkle Root	1cb965f1aaf9fb30403bdc2438f4b7958e039ccd7da0e09665b03066a5f27df2

Now lets get some information about this block. For example, the block fee, block size, and block transactions can be obtained by using `fee`, `size`, and `transactions` properties respectively on the `block` object created, as shown in the following code:

```
#!/usr/bin/env python

# import blockchain library
from blockchain import blockexplorer

# get a particular block
block =
blockexplorer.get_block('0000000000000000002e90b284607359f3415647626447643b
9b880ee00e41fa')

print("Block Fee: %s\n" % block.fee)
print("Block size: %s\n" % block.size)
print("Block transactions: %s\n" % block.transactions)

# get the latest block
block = blockexplorer.get_latest_block()
```

The following screenshot shows the block fee, block size, and block transactions output:

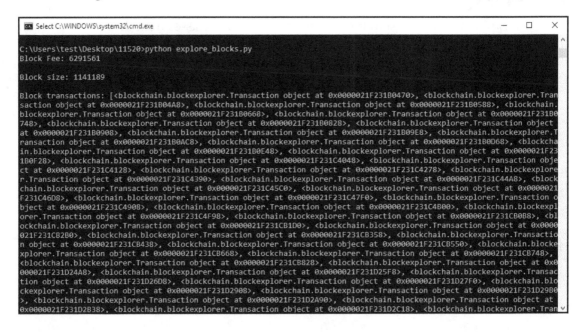

There are also many available features in the Blockchain.info library; there are a few that are more related to, for example, wallets, creating wallets, and so on.

In order to explore this library further, visit the link `https://github.com/blockchain/api-v1-client-python`.

Learning to mine bitcoin

Some features of bitcoin mining are as follows:

- Bitcoin mining is the process of adding bitcoin transactional data to bitcoin's global public ledger of past transactions. Each bitcoin miner gets involved with all the other miners in order to gather the outstanding transactions into a block by dealing with specialized analytical and arithmetical problems.

- In order to gain accuracy and solve the problems, bitcoin miners gain all of the transactions they process.
- In addition to transaction fees, miners also receive an additional reward for each block they mine. Anyone can participate in bitcoin mining by running a computer program. In addition to running on traditional computers, some companies have designed specialized bitcoin mining hardware that can process transactions and build blocks much more quickly.

One can choose to mine bitcoin in the cloud on `https://www.bitcoin.com/`.

 The course of these plans shows you that the difficulty of bitcoin mining is increasing, and getting more expensive as time goes by.

Some companies buy specialized hardware to mine bitcoin. One such piece of hardware is the 21 bitcoin computer from a company called 21.co. Hence, this hardware comes preinstalled with the necessary software.

How to mine bitcoin

There is also plenty of bitcoin mining software available, which can run on any machine. However, it may not be as efficient anymore. For example, let's go to `http://www.bitcoinx.com/bitcoin-mining-software/` for a long list of such software. They can run on all kinds of operating systems: Windows, Linux, and macOS. There are UI-based bitcoin miners, as well as command-line-based bitcoin miners—for example, Pyminer, which is an implementation in Python.

Increasing difficulty in mining bitcoin

Because of the increasing competition and difficulties, there are many factors that must be borne in mind when mining bitcoin, as shown in the following list:

- Bitcoins are getting more expensive day by day because of competition
- Many supercomputers across the globe are in competition to mine the next block and bitcoin
- As the number of bitcoin miners has increased, it has become more problematic and overpriced to start mining new bitcoin

For example, the following screenshot shows a chart of how the difficulty of bitcoin mining has been increasing; for more information refer to `https://bitcoinwisdom.com/bitcoin/difficulty`. This particular chart shows values from the last two months. This recent trend reflects the increasing difficulty that began when bitcoin was first created:

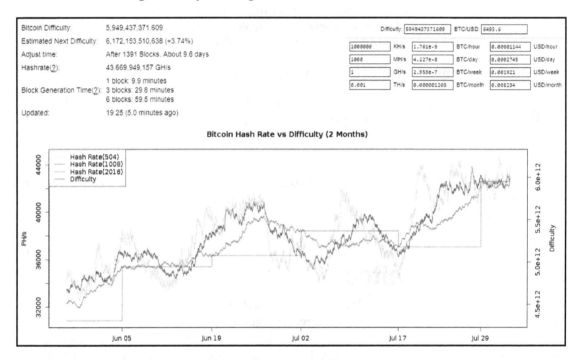

Summary

In this chapter, we learned how to get started programming bitcoin with Python. We explored Blockchain.info API programming with Python to get statistics and other bitcoin market data.

We also learned how to get started with mining bitcoin. We looked at the various ways to mine bitcoin, and we learned about why bitcoin mining may not be for everybody because of its increasing competition and difficulty.

In the next chapter, we will learn how to start running bitcoin programmatically by way of accepting bitcoin on your website, running API-based microservices, or by building a bitcoin trading bot.

3
Earning Bitcoin Programmatically

In this chapter, we will learn how to start accepting bitcoin as a payment method on our websites. We'll also learn how to build API-based microservices to earn bitcoin, and explore bitcoin trading bots.

Accepting bitcoin on your website

In this section, we will learn about the following topics:

- How to enable bitcoin payment on our websites
- Introduction to BitPay, a third-party bitcoin API service
- How to generate a bitcoin payment button
- How to add a bitcoin payment button to our website

There are a lot of third-party APIs that are available on the web that enable developers to start accepting bitcoin for products or services on their website quickly. One of the most popular ones is BitPay.

Introduction to BitPay

BitPay can be used to accept payment in a lot of different ways, including the following:

- You can use bitcoin to accept online payments on e-commerce websites
- Integrate bitcoin with a lot of different e-commerce solutions
- Integrating with shopping carts
- You can display bitcoin-enabled payment buttons, which work well for accepting donations on blogs or podcasts

How to generate a bitcoin payment button

Go through the following steps to generate a bitcoin payment button:

1. First, sign up and log in to BitPay at `https://bitpay.com/`.
2. Next, go to the **Payment Tools** | **Payment Buttons** page and create a payment button:

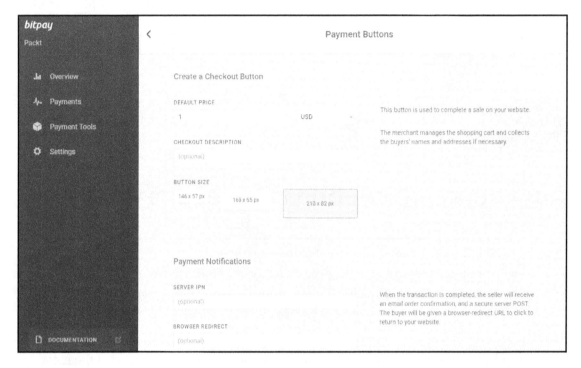

3. New fields require a **SERVER IPN** for a secure server POST, and the amount gets paid when the user clicks on it. You will see the preview of the button at the bottom of the page:

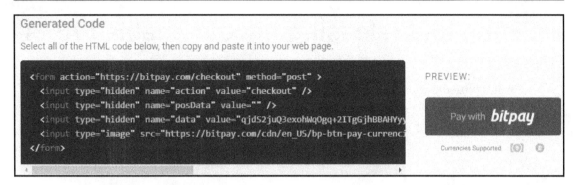

4. To add this button to the website, just copy the HTML code and paste it in the required web page.

How to add a bitcoin payment button to your website

Go through the following steps to add the payment button to your website page:

1. Open the source code of your website page in the code editor.
2. Paste the HTML code that we copied from the BitPay website in the previous section, save the file, and reload the web page.
3. The following screenshot shows the web page with a payment button that users can use to send payments:

Building and releasing bitcoin-enabled APIs

In this section, we will learn about the following topics:

- Introducing the 21.co marketplace
- Getting started with the 21.co SDK
- Starting to sell services for bitcoin

21.co marketplace

21.co is a platform that hosts a virtual marketplace where developers can create and sell microservices in return for bitcoin. For more information please refer to `https://earn.com/`.

We will demonstrate how to join this marketplace and sell microservices to earn bitcoin.

To do this, we will use 21.co's SDK.

21.co SDK

The 21.co SDK is currently supported on Ubuntu and macOS. A demonstration of Ubuntu running on AWS will be seen in this section.

You can create an AWS Ubuntu 14.x instance on AWS by following the instructions from `https://aws.amazon.com/premiumsupport/knowledge-center/create-linux-instance/`.

After creating the AWS instance, connect to it by following the instructions from the AWS documentation page at `https://docs.aws.amazon.com/AWSEC2/latest/UserGuide/AccessingInstances.html`.

Once connected to the AWS instance, install the 21.co SDK. You can do this by executing the following command:

```
curl https: //21.co | sh
```

Once the SDK is installed, log in to your 21.co account by executing the following command:

```
21 login
```

If a user does not have a 21.co login, they must create an account on the 21.co website. After logging in, first join the 21.co node to the 21.co virtual marketplace. You can do this by executing the following command:

```
21 market join
```

The status of the user's join request can be achieved by executing the following command:

```
21 market status
```

Next, test the installation by executing the following command:

```
21 doctor
```

The preceding command will show that all the tests have been passed and the node is set up and joined to the 21.co marketplace.

In order to get the bitcoin balance, execute the following command:

```
21 status
```

The preceding code shows you the bitcoin balance that is being held in the 21.co account.

Selling microservices on the 21.co marketplace

21.co's SDK comes bundled with some services. To start all of them, execute the following command:

```
21 sell start --all
```

 There might be a prompt to install a dependency. If so, you should go ahead and do it.

Sometimes, the user might need to log out and log in again to set the changes up.

For selling microservices on the 21.co marketplace, perform the following steps:

1. Execute the following command:

   ```
   21 sell start --all
   ```

   It will show you the listing of all the microservices that are available to start selling in the virtual marketplace.

2. To look at the status of your services, execute the following command:

   ```
   21 sell status
   ```

3. Once you are done with the services, or if you want to stop it, run the following command:

   ```
   21 sell stop -all
   ```

4. To look at all the activity that happened on the node, use the following command:

   ```
   21 log
   ```

This was a demonstration of how to earn bitcoin by selling and listing microservices on the 21.co marketplace.

Building a bitcoin trading bot

In this section, we will learn about the following topics:

- How to get the current bid and asking price for bitcoin
- How to make a decision whether to buy or sell bitcoin
- Triggering the bitcoin trade advice alert

 Actual buying and selling of bitcoin won't be covered, as it involves actual money. However, we will focus on sending an email alert when it is trying to buy or sell bitcoin based on the condition we set.

We will use the bitcoin price API module to fetch the bitcoin price. It is available on GitHub at https://github.com/dursk/bitcoin-price-api.

Triggering the bitcoin trade advice alert

In order to setup the bitcoin trade advice alert, go through the following steps:

1. First, start by importing the bitcoin price API, called `exchanges`:

```python
#!/usr/bin/python

# import modules
# Make sure to copy the exchanges from
https://github.com/dursk/bitcoin-price-api
# to the same location as this script
from exchanges.bitfinex import Bitfinex
```

2. Also import `smtplib`, which we will use for triggering the bitcoin price alert. Here, we define a function called `trigger_email`. We then set the server user and email details:

```python
import smtplib

# Function to send email
def trigger_email(msg):
 # Change these to your email details
 email_user = "bitcoin.harish@gmail.com"
 email_password = "bitcoin1"
 smtp_server = 'smtp.gmail.com'
 smtp_port = 587
 email_from = "bitcoin.harish@gmail.com"
 email_to = "bitcoin.harish@gmail.com"
```

3. Using `smtplib`, send the `sendmail` function to send the price alert email, as shown in the following code:

```python
# login to the email server
 server = smtplib.SMTP(smtp_server, smtp_port)
 server.starttls()
 server.login(email_user, email_password)

 # send email
 server.sendmail(email_from, email_to, msg)
 server.quit()
```

4. Next, define the buy and sell price thresholds for bitcoin. Use these thresholds to make decisions on whether to sell or buy bitcoin:

```
# define buy and sell thresholds for Bitcoin. These values you have
to change according to the current price of the bitcoin.
buy_thresh = 6500
sell_thresh = 6500
```

5. Next, we get the current bitcoin price and the current asking price for bitcoin from Bitfinex bitcoin exchange using the `exchanges` module that we imported in the `bitcoin_trade.py` script. We can also use some other exchanges, such as CoinDesk, but for the moment, we will use Bitfinex. We will get these prices in `btc_sell_price` and `btc_buy_price`.

```
# get Bitcoin prices
btc_sell_price = Bitfinex().get_current_bid()
btc_buy_price = Bitfinex().get_current_ask()
```

6. Once we have the current prices, we can compare them with the threshold prices we have set before.

7. If the buy price is lower than the sell threshold, we call the `trigger_email` function to send a buy trigger email alarm:

```
# Trigger Buy email if buy price is lower than threshold
if btc_buy_price < buy_thresh:
email_msg = """
 Bitcoin Buy Price is %s which is lower than
 threshold price of %s.
 Good time to buy!""" % (btc_buy_price, buy_thresh)

trigger_email(email_msg)
```

8. If the sell price is greater than the sell threshold, we call the `trigger_email` function to send the sell trigger email alert:

```
# Trigger sell email if sell price is higher than threshold
if btc_sell_price > sell_thresh:

  email_msg = """
 Bitcoin sell Price is %s which is higher than
 threshold price of %s.
 Good time to sell!""" % (btc_sell_price, sell_thresh)

trigger_email(email_msg)
```

How to get a current bid and asking price for bitcoin

Google search is the simplest way to search for the current bid rate. In order to achieve the buying and selling of bitcoin, the triggering of both should be done accordingly.

The triggering of buy bitcoin

The following are the steps to go through to get the current bid:

1. First, check the bitcoin price online.
2. Modify the script so that the buy alert triggers first. Set the buy threshold to higher than the current price. Here, we set the buy threshold to 6500, as shown in the following code:

```
# define buy and sell thresholds for Bitcoin
buy_thresh = 6500
sell_thresh = 6500
```

3. Save the script and execute it. The following screenshot shows the executed script:

```
C:\Users\test\Desktop\11520>python bitcoin_trade.py
C:\Users\test\Desktop\11520>_
```

The script has been executed and the buy alert should have gone. Check it in the email.

The following screenshot shows that we have received the bitcoin alert email advising us to buy bitcoin, according to the criteria that we have set up in the script:

```
Bitcoin Buy Price is 6416.5 which is lower then
threshhold price of 6500.
Good time to buy!
```

The triggering of sell bitcoin

1. Initially, we should set the sell threshold as lower than the current price. So, for example, let's set the threshold for `6400` and execute the script again. The following code shows that the `sell_thresh` is set to `6400`:

```
# define buy and sell thresholds for bitcoin
buy_thresh = 6400
sell_thresh = 6400
```

   Now, the sell alert should execute. Verify it in the email again.

2. After verifying this, we should see that we have received the email alert advising us to sell bitcoin because the current asking price is higher than what we are willing to sell for:

   ```
   Bitcoin sell Price is 6420.4 which is higher then
   threshhold price of 6400.
   Good time to sell!
   ```

3. The script is ready. You can now set it to run automatically on all kinds of operating systems. On Windows, use the **Task Scheduler**.

4. From the **Action** menu, choose **Create Task...**, and give it the name `Bitcoin trade alert`, as shown in the following screenshot:

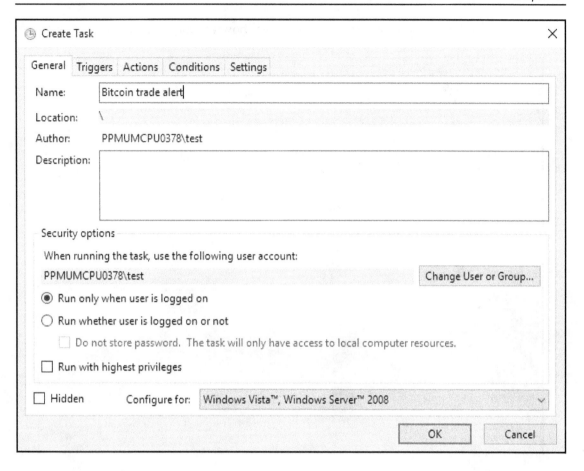

5. From the **Triggers** tab, click on **New...**, as shown in the following screenshot:

6. Choose the **Daily** radio button.

7. Then, in **Advanced settings**, choose to repeat the task after the required number of minutes or hours. Here, we will set it to every 1 hour, as shown in the following screenshot:

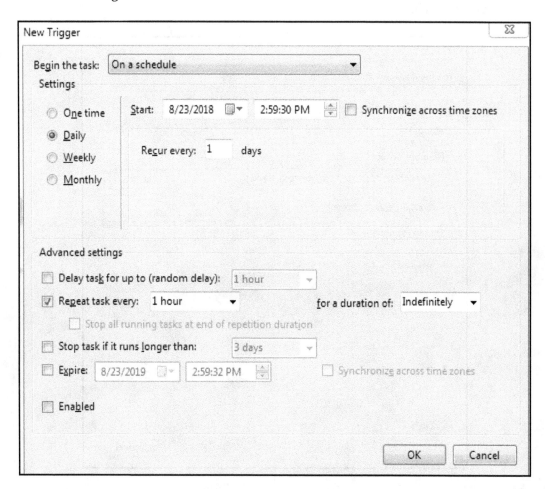

8. Next, from the **Actions** tab, click on the **New...** button.

9. Choose the script that was created to be executed whenever the task runs by clicking on the **Browse...** button. Now, this task will run automatically every hour, and will check for bitcoin prices and send an email advising us whether to buy or sell bitcoin.

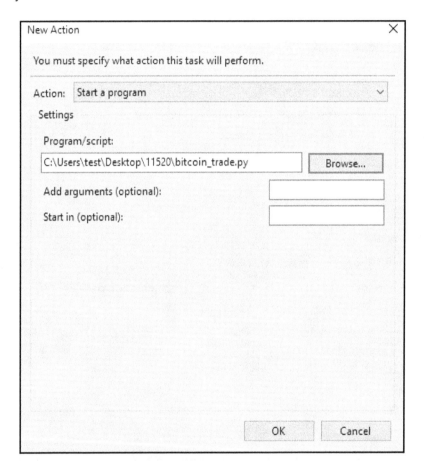

You can also choose to trigger the trade right from the script itself, using any of the bitcoin exchange APIs, such as coinbase.com. As it involves actual money, the user needs to be careful with it.

Summary

In this chapter, we explored how to enable bitcoin payments on a website, introduced you to BitPay, learned about how to generate a bitcoin payment button, and how to add the payment button to our websites. We also introduced the 21.co marketplace and buying/selling services for bitcoin, as well as writing a bare bones bitcoin trading bot. We learned how to get the current bidding and asking prices for bitcoin. We also learned how to decide as to whether to buy or sell bitcoins, as well as how to send out an email alert advising us whether to execute that thread.

In the next chapter, we will learn about performing data analysis on bitcoin data.

4
Bitcoin Data Analysis

In this chapter, we will explore the manipulation and visualization of bitcoin price data using Python. We will also explore bitcoin transaction graphs, along with collecting and analyzing *Bitcoin Dice* game data using Python.

Manipulating and visualizing bitcoin price data

In this section, we will introduce the following topics:

- Getting set up for data analysis
- Getting, reading in, and cleaning bitcoin price data
- Exploring, manipulating, and visualizing the cleaned-up data

 We first need to install several Python libraries, which includes installing the pandas module for reading in data, and also doing some exploratory analysis. We'll also be installing matplotlib for creating plots and charts, as well as Jupyter Notebooks, as they are the best for this kind of work involving data analysis.

Getting set up for data analysis

To install the Python modules, open the command-line program. In the command line, to install pandas, execute the following command:

```
pip install pandas
```

Similarly, to install matplotlib, execute the following command:

```
pip install matplotlib
```

To install Jupyter, execute the following command:

```
pip install jupyter
```

Having finished installing the required modules, launch the Jupyter Notebook by executing the `jupyter notebook` command. This will open up a new browser window, or a tab, where it will display the list of files that are already there from the folder where we executed the `jupyter notebook` command. The following screenshot shows the `jupyter notebook` command:

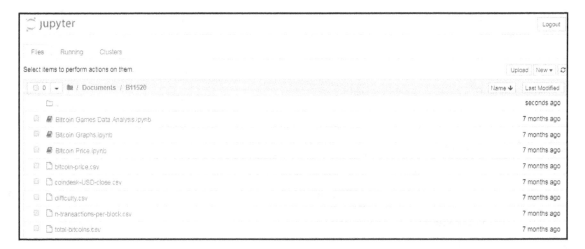

Next, choose to create a new Python 3 notebook, as shown in the following screenshot:

Getting, reading in, and cleaning bitcoin price data

We will start by importing the necessary modules.

Import `pandas` to enable you to read in the data and start exploring it. The following screenshot shows the `import pandas` command:

Also, import `matplotlib` for drawing plots from the data.

We need to set some options for `pandas` and `matplotlib`. The following screenshot shows the command for importing `matplotlib`:

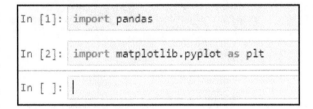

The first option we will set is called `options.mode.chained_assignment = None`.

 The preceding option is to make sure that the operations are for the cleanup, which will be performed on the pandas DataFrame objects; we want the cleanup to happen on the original DataFrame objects and not on copies.

The following screenshot shows the `options.mode.chained_assignment =`
`None` option:

```
In [5]: import pandas as pd

In [6]: import matplotlib.pyplot as plt

In [7]: pd.options.mode.chained_assignment = None

In [ ]:
```

Also, set `matplotlib` to visualize and display all the charts shown in the following
screenshot:

```
In [5]: import pandas as pd

In [6]: import matplotlib.pyplot as plt

In [7]: pd.options.mode.chained_assignment = None

In [8]: %matplotlib inline

In [ ]: |
```

The price data we have is from `coindesk.com`, as shown in the following screenshot, and
it is freely available for download:

Download the data in CSV format and read this data using pandas. This is a CSV file, so we will use the read_csv method from pandas, as shown in the following screenshot:

```
In [5]:  import pandas as pd

In [6]:  import matplotlib.pyplot as plt

In [7]:  pd.options.mode.chained_assignment = None

In [8]:  %matplotlib inline

In [9]:  price = pd.read_csv "D:/bitcoin-price.csv"

In [ ]:  |
```

DataFrame

The data in a pandas data object is called a DataFrame. A DataFrame is in a tabular data format. Now, print out some records to see how this looks. To print this out, we can call a method called `head()` on the price DataFrame.

When we do this, we get two columns—`Date` and `Close Price`—for the bitcoin in USD for that day. We also have a default index for the rows starting from 0, which was inserted by pandas by default while reading in the data. The following screenshot shows the two columns, `Date` and `Close Price`:

To get top-level information about this data, call the `info()` method on it. After calling this method, we get 2,592 records. There are two columns: `Date` and `Close Price`. `Date` has 2,592 non-null records of the `type` object, which means that the `Date` field has been read as text. We would have to change it to a proper date-time format later. We have the close price as a numeric float type. It has 2,590 non-null records, which are two records fewer than the `Date` field.

The following screenshot shows the details of the `info()` method:

```
In [5]:  import pandas as pd

In [6]:  import matplotlib.pyplot as plt

In [7]:  pd.options.mode.chained_assignment = None

In [8]:  %matplotlib inline

In [9]:  price = pd.read_csv("D:/bitcoin-price.csv")

In [10]: price.head()
Out[10]:
                              Date    Close Price

         0   2010-07-18 00:00:00           0.09

         1   2010-07-19 00:00:00           0.08

         2   2010-07-20 00:00:00           0.07

         3   2010-07-21 00:00:00           0.08

         4   2010-07-22 00:00:00           0.05

In [11]: price.info
         <class 'pandas.core.frame.DataFrame'>
         RangeIndex: 2592 entries, 0 to 2591
         Data columns (total 2 columns):
         Date            2592 non-null object
         Close Price     2590 non-null float64
         dtypes: float64(1), object(1)
         memory usage: 40.6+ KB
```

In order to print for the records from bottom, call the `tail()` method. This method shows that the last two records should not exist, as they are not a date or price. We need to remove these before proceeding with further analysis.

We can see that the close price has NaN values, which means that it has missing values. We can use this factor to remove these two records from the DataFrame. We call drop any method on the price, which will remove the records that have one or more of the columns as null or missing values.

Bear in mind that we are just removing it from the DataFrame price and not from the CSV file from which we read the data.

The code in the following screenshot shows the `tail()` method implementation:

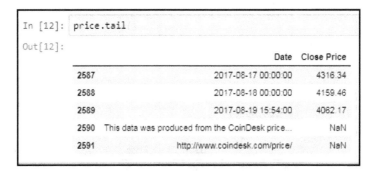

Also, look at the bottom rows again to see if the records we wanted to remove have been removed. We can see in the following screenshot that they have, in fact, been removed:

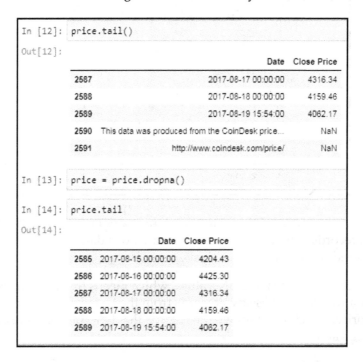

Data cleanup

Another data cleaning task we need to do is convert the `Date` column from an object or text format to a date-time format. We use the pandas `to_datetime` method to do this.

Here, we ask the `to_datetime` method to convert the `Date` field or `price` DataFrame, and we also supply the format. We then assign the `Date` field back to the DataFrame, as shown in the following screenshot:

```
In [15]:  price['Date'] = pd.to_datetime price['Date'], format = "%Y-%m-%d"

In [ ]:  |
```

This is the reason that we set the chained assignment as equal to `null` earlier, because we wanted to make the changes back on the original DataFrame.

Call the `info()` method again to see whether the data cleanup has an impact. We can see that the `Date` field is now in a date-time format, as we wanted, and there are no non-null records in the data, as shown in the following screenshot:

```
In [15]:  price['Date'] = pd.to_datetime(price['Date'], format = "%Y-%m-%d")

In [16]:  price.info

          <class 'pandas.core.frame.DataFrame'>
          Int64Index: 2590 entries, 0 to 2589
          Data columns (total 2 columns):
          Date           2590 non-null datetime64[ns]
          Close Price    2590 non-null float64
          dtypes: datetime64[ns](1), float64(1)
          memory usage: 60.7 KB
```

Setting the index to the Date column

We also need to set the index to the `Date` column and remove the `Date` column as a separate column. This will help us to run some interesting queries on the date data.

The code in the following screenshot shows how to set the index to the `Date` column:

```
In [14]: price.tail()
Out[14]:
                          Date   Close Price
         2585  2017-08-15 00:00:00     4204.43
         2586  2017-08-16 00:00:00     4425.30
         2587  2017-08-17 00:00:00     4316.34
         2588  2017-08-18 00:00:00     4159.46
         2589  2017-08-19 15:54:00     4062.17

In [15]: price['Date'] = pd.to_datetime(price['Date'], format = "%Y-%m-%d")

In [16]: price.info()
         <class 'pandas.core.frame.DataFrame'>
         Int64Index: 2590 entries, 0 to 2589
         Data columns (total 2 columns):
         Date           2590 non-null datetime64[ns]
         Close Price    2590 non-null float64
         dtypes: datetime64[ns](1), float64(1)
         memory usage: 60.7 KB

In [17]: price.index = price "Date"
```

Next, delete the `Date` column as a separate column, since it is already set up as an index, as shown in the following screenshot:

```
In [17]: price.index = price["Date"]

In [18]: del price "Date"
```

Now, the `Date` column can be seen as an index and not a separate column anymore, as shown in the following screenshot:

Exploring, manipulating, and visualizing the cleaned-up data

As the data cleanup is done, start with the data exploration tasks. We can use the pandas date-time capabilities to run some interesting queries.

For example, if we want to get all the records from a particular year, pass that year to the DataFrame inside square brackets. The following screenshot shows the price data from the year 2010:

```
In [20]: price '2010'
Out[20]:
```

	Close Price
Date	
2010-07-18	0.09
2010-07-19	0.08
2010-07-20	0.07
2010-07-21	0.08
2010-07-22	0.05
2010-07-23	0.06
2010-07-24	0.05
2010-07-25	0.05
2010-07-26	0.06
2010-07-27	0.06
2010-07-28	0.06
2010-07-29	0.07
2010-07-30	0.06
2010-07-31	0.07
2010-08-01	0.06
2010-08-02	0.06
2010-08-03	0.06
2010-08-04	0.06
2010-08-05	0.06
2010-08-06	0.06
2010-08-07	0.06
2010-08-08	0.06

We can also specify whether we want the data from a particular date.

The following screenshot shows the bitcoin price in USD from August 1, 2017:

```
In [21]: price '2017-08-01'
Out[21]:
                    Close Price
         Date

         2017-08-01      2735.59
```

We can also specify whether we want the data from a particular period spanning certain dates.

The following screenshot shows the data from August 1, 2017, onward:

```
In [22]: price '2017-08-01':
Out[22]:
                              Close Price
         Date

         2017-08-01 00:00:00      2735.59
         2017-08-02 00:00:00      2723.58
         2017-08-03 00:00:00      2814.36
         2017-08-04 00:00:00      2883.68
         2017-08-05 00:00:00      3301.76
         2017-08-06 00:00:00      3255.00
         2017-08-07 00:00:00      3431.97
         2017-08-08 00:00:00      3453.16
         2017-08-09 00:00:00      3377.54
         2017-08-10 00:00:00      3445.28
         2017-08-11 00:00:00      3679.61
         2017-08-12 00:00:00      3917.65
         2017-08-13 00:00:00      4111.20
         2017-08-14 00:00:00      4382.74
         2017-08-15 00:00:00      4204.43
         2017-08-16 00:00:00      4425.30
         2017-08-17 00:00:00      4316.34
         2017-08-18 00:00:00      4159.46
         2017-08-19 15:54:00      4062.17
```

Statistical information can also be retrieved using pandas methods. For example, to get the minimum price from this dataset, we can use the `min()` method, as shown in the following screenshot:

```
In [23]:  price.min

Out[23]:  Close Price     0.05
          dtype: float64
```

To get the maximum price, use the `max ()` method, as shown in the following screenshot:

```
In [24]:  price.max

Out[24]:  Close Price     4425.3
          dtype: float64
```

A whole bunch of statistical information can be received in one go using the `describe ()` method, as shown in the following screenshot:

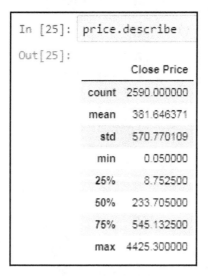

```
In [25]:  price.describe

Out[25]:
                    Close Price

          count   2590.000000
          mean     381.646371
           std     570.770109
           min       0.050000
           25%       8.752500
           50%     233.705000
           75%     545.132500
           max    4425.300000
```

Data visualization

It is very easy to start creating plots from data using `pandas` and `matplotlib`. To plot the entirety of the data, we will call the `plot` method on the `price DataFrame`, and we will get a plot where the *x* axis is the date and the *y* axis is the price data.

The following screenshot describes the plot, wherein the *x* axis is the date and the *y* axis is the price data:

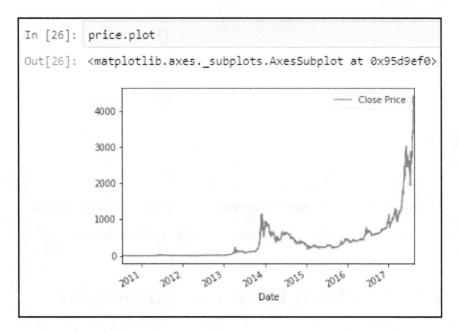

We can also zoom in on a certain time period. For example, in order to plot the data from 2017 only, first select the data that is from 2017 and then call the `plot ()` method on the subset of data.

In the following screenshot, we have a plot for the price data from 2017 onward:

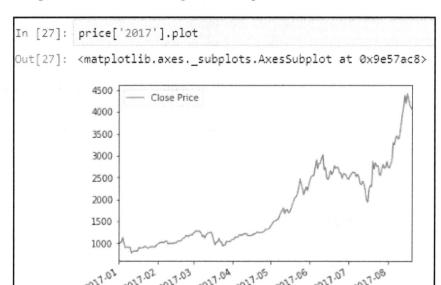

In the next section, we will look at how to use bitcoin transaction graphs.

Exploring bitcoin transaction graphs

In this section, we will learn about how to get the blockchain data, and provide step-by-step information as to how to explore, clean up, analyze, and visualize this data.

Bitcoin and blockchain graphs

`Blockchain.info` is one of the best places to look at the latest bitcoin stats and graphs. There are different kinds of charts and graphs concerning bitcoin and blockchain that are available for analysis. We can also download the data in a variety of formats—CSV, JSON, and so on. We have downloaded some of this data in CSV format in the previous section, and now we will explore this data in a Jupyter Notebook.

We start by importing the modules we need. We need `pandas` for data reading, exploration, and cleanup, and we need `matplotlib` for creating the graphs.

Look at the data showing the total number of bitcoins in circulation. Read the CSV file that has this data and create a `pandas DataFrame`.

The following screenshot shows the data for the total number of bitcoins in circulation:

Import Modules

```
In [1]:  import pandas as pd
         import matplotlib.pyplot as plt

         pd.options.mode.chained_assignment = None
         %matplotlib inline
```

Dataset

Dataset used in this notebook are from blockchain.info

Example 1 - Total Bitcoins

Read in the data

```
In [2]:  bitcoins = pd.read_csv("total-bitcoins.csv", header=None, names=['Date', 'Bitcoins'])
```

Explore data

```
In [3]:  bitcoins.head()
```

Out[3]:

	Date	Bitcoins
0	2016-08-28 00:00:00	15841112.5
1	2016-08-29 00:00:00	15842975.0
2	2016-08-30 00:00:00	15845025.0
3	2016-08-31 00:00:00	15846700.0
4	2016-09-01 00:00:00	15848450.0

Exploring, cleaning up, and analyzing data

In order to explore this data, we use the `head()` method to look at the records from the top and we call the `info()` method on the DataFrame to get some more information, such as how many records there are, how many null or missing records there are, or what the data types of the various columns are.

We can see that the `Date` column is shown as object. We change this to date-time to visualize this data. To do this, we use the `to_datetime` method, and assign the converted values back to the same column—the DataFrame.

The following screenshot depicts the date format of bitcoins:

```
         Explore data

In [3]:  bitcoins.head()

Out[3]:              Date      Bitcoins

         0   2016-08-28 00:00:00   15841112.5

         1   2016-08-29 00:00:00   15842975.0

         2   2016-08-30 00:00:00   15845025.0

         3   2016-08-31 00:00:00   15846700.0

         4   2016-09-01 00:00:00   15848450.0


In [4]:  bitcoins.info()

         <class 'pandas.core.frame.DataFrame'>
         RangeIndex: 364 entries, 0 to 363
         Data columns (total 2 columns):
         Date        364 non-null object
         Bitcoins    364 non-null float64
         dtypes: float64(1), object(1)
         memory usage: 5.8+ KB


         Cleanup and manipulate data

In [5]:  bitcoins["Date"] = pd.to_datetime(bitcoins["Date"], format="%Y-%m-%d")

In [6]:  bitcoins.index = bitcoins['Date']
         del bitcoins['Date']
         bitcoins.head()
```

Set the index of the DataFrame to the `Date` column and delete the `Date` column as a separate column. Perform this step in order to take advantage of the time series features of pandas.

Now, check again whether the changes took place by calling `info` and `head` on the DataFrame.

The following screenshot shows the bitcoins for a particular range of dates:

```
In [6]: bitcoins.index = bitcoins['Date']
        del bitcoins['Date']
        bitcoins.head |

Out[6]:              Bitcoins

            Date

        2016-08-28   15841112.5

        2016-08-29   15842975.0

        2016-08-30   15845025.0

        2016-08-31   15846700.0

        2016-09-01   15848450.0


In [7]: bitcoins.info()

        <class 'pandas.core.frame.DataFrame'>
        DatetimeIndex: 364 entries, 2016-08-28 to 2017-08-26
        Data columns (total 1 columns):
        Bitcoins    364 non-null float64
        dtypes: float64(1)
        memory usage: 5.7 KB


In [8]: bitcoins.head()

Out[8]:              Bitcoins

            Date

        2016-08-28   15841112.5

        2016-08-29   15842975.0

        2016-08-30   15845025.0

        2016-08-31   15846700.0

        2016-09-01   15848450.0
```

We are now ready to create a graph from this data. Call the `plot ()` method on the DataFrame and then call the `show ()` method to display the graph.

It shows the total number of bitcoins that have already been mined over the time period for which we have this record.

The following screenshot describes the graph for the preceding data:

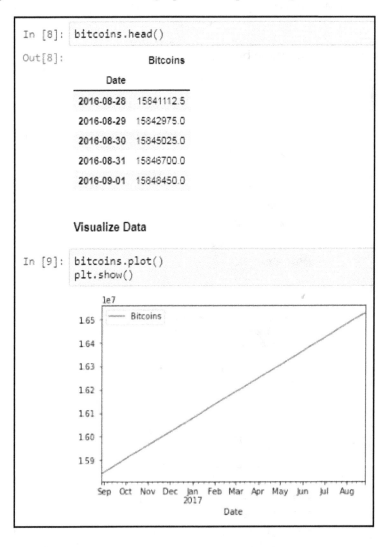

Visualizing data

Let's look at another example. Here, we are looking at transactions for block data that we read into the data:

Example 2 - Transactions per block

Read in the data

```
In [10]:  transactions = pd.read_csv("n-transactions-per-block.csv", header=None, names=['Date', 'Transactions'])
```

Initially, we visually explore this data using the head and info methods, as shown in the following screenshot:

Explore data

```
In [11]:  transactions.head()
```

Out[11]:

	Date	Transactions
0	2016-08-28 00:00:00	1147.953947
1	2016-08-29 00:00:00	1511.959732
2	2016-08-30 00:00:00	1542.339394
3	2016-08-31 00:00:00	1676.866667
4	2016-09-01 00:00:00	1689.411348

```
In [12]:  bitcoins.info()

          <class 'pandas.core.frame.DataFrame'>
          DatetimeIndex: 364 entries, 2016-08-28 to 2017-08-26
          Data columns (total 1 columns):
          Bitcoins    364 non-null float64
          dtypes: float64(1)
          memory usage: 5.7 KB
```

Next, we clean up, convert, and reshape the data, as shown in the following screenshot:

Cleanup and manipulate data

```
In [13]:  transactions["Date"] = pd.to_datetime(transactions["Date"], format="%Y-%m-%d")
          transactions.index = transactions['Date']
          del transactions['Date']
```

Finally, we visualize our transactions in the block data, as shown in the following screenshot:

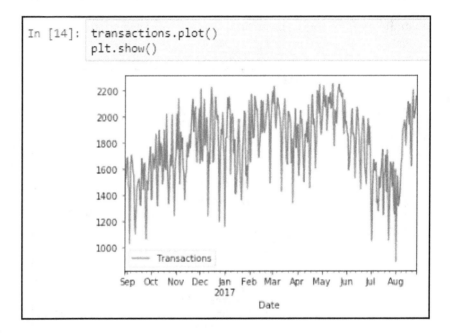

```
In [14]:  transactions.plot()
          plt.show()
```

Similarly, there is another example that we should look at regarding the data showing mining difficulty. The steps for mining data are as follows:

1. Read in the data, as shown in the following screenshot:

Read in the data

```
In [15]:  difficulty = pd.read_csv("difficulty.csv", header=None, names=['Date', 'Difficulty'])
```

---

2. Explore the data, as shown in the following screenshot:

Explore data

```
In [16]: difficulty.head()
```

```
Out[16]:              Date        Difficulty

         0  2016-08-28 00:00:00  2.173755e+11

         1  2016-08-29 00:00:00  2.184418e+11

         2  2016-08-30 00:00:00  2.207559e+11

         3  2016-08-31 00:00:00  2.207559e+11

         4  2016-09-01 00:00:00  2.207559e+11
```

```
In [17]: difficulty.info()

         <class 'pandas.core.frame.DataFrame'>
         RangeIndex: 364 entries, 0 to 363
         Data columns (total 2 columns):
         Date          364 non-null object
         Difficulty    364 non-null float64
         dtypes: float64(1), object(1)
         memory usage: 5.8+ KB
```

3. Clean up the data, as shown in the following screenshot:

Cleanup and manipulate data

```
In [18]: difficulty["Date"] = pd.to_datetime(difficulty["Date"], format="%Y-%m-%d")
         difficulty.index = difficulty['Date']
         del difficulty['Date']
```

4. Finally, visualize the data, as shown in the following screenshot:

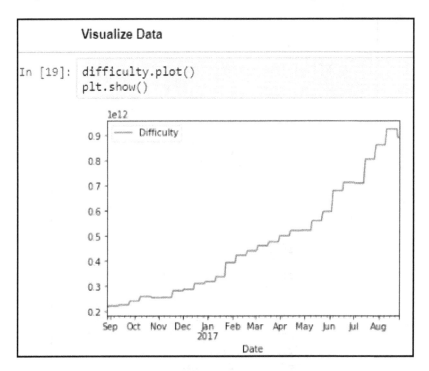

We can see that there has been a gradual increase in mining difficulty over the years, and it trends upwards. These are just a few examples of transaction graphs. There is a lot of other data available for you to explore from the bitcoin and blockchain ecosystem.

In the next module, we will look at how to collect and analyze *Bitcoin Dice* game data.

Collecting and analyzing Bitcoin Dice game data

In this section, we will look at the data from a dice games portal, read in the data from the API, and use `pandas` to convert it into a tabular format. We will also export the data and find the things that need cleaning up. We'll clean up, manipulate, and reshape the data, making it ready for analysis, and finally, we will draw a simple plot from the clean data.

Getting data from the Games Web API

The user can explore the dice games data from MegaDice.com, which is available from the website's API link at `https://www.megadice.com`.

We will use the `pandas read_JSON` method to read individual winner history data from the MegaDice API link. We create a `pandas DataFrame`, called `leaders`, from this data and call in the `head ()` method to see what this data looks like.

The code in the following screenshots shows the creation of the `pandas DataFrame`, `leaders`:

Read in the data

```
In [2]: leaders = pd.read_json('https://session.megadice.com/globalstats/leaderBoardWinners/')
```

Explore data

```
In [3]: leaders.head()
```

Out[3]:

	2014-11-05	2014-11-06
longesWinStreakPrizeInSatoshis	125000000	20000000
longestWinNick	dooglus	leen
longestWinStreakWinnerHash	6848acbf6de4f8e9170bd9d1e28008e5	7ef585ba27ad8eea00d509622570e2d3 7ef585ba27ad8eea00d509
mostProfitNick	eleph	Throne
mostProfitPrizeInSatoshis	100000000	20000000

5 rows × 708 columns

The data we have imported has 703 columns, most of which are individual dates. We will delete the last column, **queryTimeInSeconds**, which is not really part of the actual data, and should not be there. This column is shown in the following screenshot:

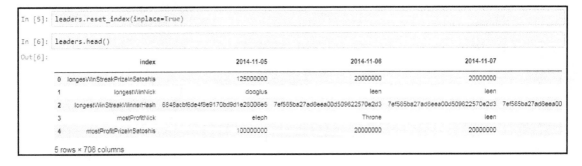

As there are too many columns and very few rows, we want the columns to be rows, where each state has a single row of records. In order to perform this, we need to flip the columns to rows and vice versa. To do this, we need to go through the following steps:

1. First, we reset the index so that we bring in the current index as another column. The values for this column will become column names when we flip the DataFrame. Confirm it with the head () method, as shown in the following screenshot:

```
In [5]: leaders.reset_index(inplace=True)
```

```
In [6]: leaders.head()
```

Out[6]:

	index	2014-11-05	2014-11-06	2014-11-07
0	longestWinStreakPrizeInSatoshis	125000000	20000000	20000000
1	longestWinNick	dooglus	leen	leen
2	longestWinStreakWinnerHash	6848acbf6de4f8e9170bd9d1e28006e5	7ef585ba27ad8eea00d509622570e2d3	7ef585ba27ad8eea00d509622570e2d3	7ef585ba27ad8eea00
3	mostProfitNick	eleph	Throne	leen
4	mostProfitPrizeInSatoshis	100000000	20000000	20000000

5 rows × 708 columns

2. Next, flip the DataFrame by using a method called T, or transposed, which can be seen in the following screenshot:

```
In [7]: leaders2 = leaders.set_index('index').T
```

3. Now, in the following screenshot, we can see that our row index has become dates and our earlier rows have become columns:

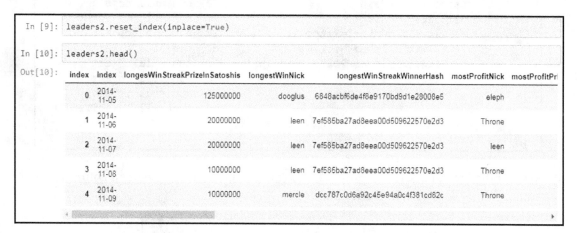

```
In [8]:  leaders2.head()
```

Out[8]:	index	longesWinStreakPrizeInSatoshis	longestWinNick	longestWinStreakWinnerHash	mostProfitNick	mostProfitPrizeInSatoshis	mostProfitWir
	2014-11-05	125000000	dooglus	6848acbf6de4f8e9170bd9d1e28008e5	eleph	100000000	bd8ecf07a31ac12466871227
	2014-11-06	20000000	leen	7ef585ba27ad8eea00d509622570e2d3	Throne	20000000	73ffa73301d1df899c6c4a8d
	2014-11-07	20000000	leen	7ef585ba27ad8eea00d509622570e2d3	leen	20000000	7ef585ba27ad8eea00d50962
	2014-11-08	10000000	leen	7ef585ba27ad8eea00d509622570e2d3	Throne	10000000	73ffa73301d1df899c6c4a8d
	2014-11-09	10000000	mercle	dcc787c0d6a92c45e94a0c4f381cd82c	Throne	10000000	73ffa73301d1df899c6c4a8d

We've got the columns and rows we want, but there are also a few other things that need to be done. We want the date values to be in a date-time format, but currently it is in text format. However, the transposing of the DataFrame has changed the date values into an index. We need to first convert them into a column using the `reset_index` method, as shown in the following screenshot:

```
In [9]:  leaders2.reset_index(inplace=True)

In [10]:  leaders2.head()
```

Out[10]:	index	index	longesWinStreakPrizeInSatoshis	longestWinNick	longestWinStreakWinnerHash	mostProfitNick	mostProfitPri
	0	2014-11-05	125000000	dooglus	6848acbf6de4f8e9170bd9d1e28008e5	eleph	
	1	2014-11-06	20000000	leen	7ef585ba27ad8eea00d509622570e2d3	Throne	
	2	2014-11-07	20000000	leen	7ef585ba27ad8eea00d509622570e2d3	leen	
	3	2014-11-08	10000000	leen	7ef585ba27ad8eea00d509622570e2d3	Throne	
	4	2014-11-09	10000000	mercle	dcc787c0d6a92c45e94a0c4f381cd82c	Throne	

Now we can convert this text data into a proper date-time format, as shown in the following screenshot:

```
In [11]:  leaders2["Date"] = pd.to_datetime(leaders2["index"], format="%Y-%m-%d")
```

Call the `info ()` method to confirm this. We have the new column `Date` in the proper date-time format. Date values are required to be in text format in the column name index, as shown in the following screenshot:

```
In [12]:  leaders2.info()

          <class 'pandas.core.frame.DataFrame'>
          RangeIndex: 707 entries, 0 to 706
          Data columns (total 17 columns):
          index                              707 non-null object
          longesWinStreakPrizeInSatoshis     707 non-null object
          longestWinNick                     671 non-null object
          longestWinStreakWinnerHash         707 non-null object
          mostProfitNick                     695 non-null object
          mostProfitPrizeInSatoshis          707 non-null object
          mostProfitWinnerHash               707 non-null object
          mostWonNick                        697 non-null object
          mostWonPrizeInSatoshis             707 non-null object
          mostWonWinnerHash                  707 non-null object
          unlikliestWinNick                  700 non-null object
          unlikliestWinPrizeInSatoshis       707 non-null object
          unlikliestWinStreakNick            675 non-null object
          unlikliestWinStreakPrizeInSatoshis 707 non-null object
          unlikliestWinStreakWinnerHash      707 non-null object
          unlikliestWinWinnerHash            707 non-null object
          Date                               707 non-null datetime64[ns]
          dtypes: datetime64[ns](1), object(16)
          memory usage: 94.0+ KB
```

We will set the index back to the proper `Date` column and remove the `Date` column as a separate column, as shown in the following screenshot:

```
In [13]:  leaders2.index = leaders2['Date']
          del leaders2['Date']
          del leaders2['index']
```

Now, we have the DataFrame properly indexed on the `Date` field:

In [14]:	leaders2.head()						
Out[14]:	index	longesWinStreakPrizeInSatoshis	longestWinNick	longestWinStreakWinnerHash	mostProfitNick	mostProfitPrizeInSatoshis	mostProfitWir
	Date						
	2014-11-05	125000000	dooglus	6848acbf6de4f6e9170bd9d1e28008e5	eleph	100000000	bd8ecf07a31ac12466871227
	2014-11-06	20000000	leen	7ef585ba27ad8eea00d509622570e2d3	Throne	20000000	73ffa73301d1df899c6c4a8d
	2014-11-07	20000000	leen	7ef585ba27ad8eea00d509622570e2d3	leen	20000000	7ef585ba27ad8eea00d50962
	2014-11-08	10000000	leen	7ef585ba27ad8eea00d509622570e2d3	Throne	10000000	73ffa73301d1df899c6c4a8d
	2014-11-09	10000000	mercle	dcc787c0d6a92c45e94a0c4f381cd82c	Throne	10000000	73ffa73301d1df899c6c4a8d

Draw a sample plot of this data using the `plot ()` method and show it with the `plt.show ()` method, as shown in the following screenshot:

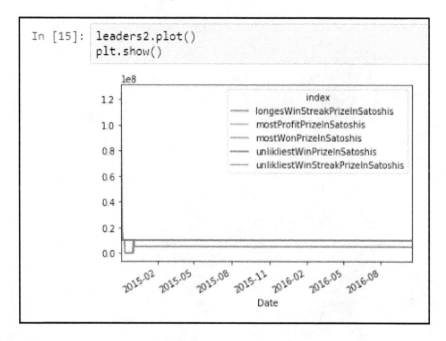

Now this data can be used as `pandas` time series functions, or multiple blocks that can be visualized for different subsets of dates, and so on.

Summary

In this chapter, we learned how to prepare our setup for data analysis. We saw how to get, read in, and clean the price data. We also learned how to explore, manipulate, and visualize the cleaned-up data.

We also explored some of the bitcoin and blockchain graphs that we can create. We learned where to get the relevant data, and we read this data in a Jupyter Notebook and imported the necessary modules. We cleaned up and manipulated this data, and finally, we created graphs out of this data and a notebook, but without using Python.

We also explored the data from a dice games portal. We added the data from the API and used pandas to convert it into a tabular format. We explored the data and found the things that needed cleaning up. We cleaned up and manipulated the data and made it ready for analysis.

Other Books You May Enjoy

If you enjoyed this book, you may be interested in these other books by Packt:

Blockchain Quick Reference
Brenn Hill, Samanyu Chopra, Paul Valencourt

ISBN: 9781788995788

- Understand how blockchain architecture components work
- Acquaint yourself with cryptography and the mechanics behind blockchain
- Apply consensus protocol to determine the business sustainability
- Understand what ICOs and crypto-mining are and how they work
- Create cryptocurrency wallets and coins for transaction mechanisms
- Understand the use of Ethereum for smart contract and DApp development

Ethereum Projects for Beginners
Kenny Vaneetvelde

ISBN: 9781789537406

- Develop your ideas fast and efficiently using the Ethereum blockchain
- Make writing and deploying smart contracts easy and manageable
- Work with private data in blockchain applications
- Handle large files in blockchain applications
- Ensure your decentralized applications are safe
- Explore how Ethereum development frameworks work
- Create your own cryptocurrency or token on the Ethereum blockchain
- Make sure your cryptocurrency is ERC20-compliant to launch an ICO

Leave a review - let other readers know what you think

Please share your thoughts on this book with others by leaving a review on the site that you bought it from. If you purchased the book from Amazon, please leave us an honest review on this book's Amazon page. This is vital so that other potential readers can see and use your unbiased opinion to make purchasing decisions, we can understand what our customers think about our products, and our authors can see your feedback on the title that they have worked with Packt to create. It will only take a few minutes of your time, but is valuable to other potential customers, our authors, and Packt. Thank you!

Index

www.ingramcontent.com/pod-product-compliance
Lightning Source LLC
Chambersburg PA
CBHW080542060326
40690CB00022B/5205